MY DIET IS WORKING! – WHEN TRAVELING

RELEASE NEGATIVE ENERGY TO REACH YOUR HEALTHY WEIGHT

(#1 in a series by *Slender Suggestions*)

SS

by ROGER THIEL

MY DIET IS WORKING! – WHEN TRAVELING

RELEASE NEGATIVE ENERGY TO REACH YOUR HEALTHY WEIGHT

www.MyDietIsWorking.com

SS

(#1 in a series by *Slender Suggestions*)
– by Thiel Press –
1101 – 14th Street, N.W., #64, Washington, D.C. 20005

Copyright © 2018 by Roger N. Thiel

ISBN 978-0-9976605-3-1

WASHINGTON, D.C.
Established 1974

table of CONTENTS

My Diet Is Working! – When Traveling

Angels fly, because they take themselves lightly.

58 ILLUSTRATED WHOLE-PAGE INSIGHTS – INCLUDING THESE THEMES: Visiting Locations Where I Have a History – Meals With Other People – Recovering From a "Food Setback" – Is This Me, Succeeding? – Visiting Family, Friends and Associates – Holidays – Convenience, Processed and Packaged Foods – Parties – I am Already Full!

- **5** — Introduction – The "Other Ninety Percent" Of Positive Body Change
- **19** — "Clean Out The Basement"
- **31** — Make Friends With Repeated Energy
- **43** — Try A "Bigger Shovel"
- **57** — Your Further Resources
- **71** —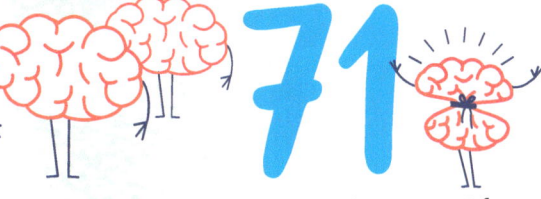
- **71** — CONCLUSION -- The Rest Of Your Life -- Make Friends With Exercise Or Physical Activity
- **72** — Acknowledgements & About The Author
- **73** — Coming Editions Of My Diet Is Working!
- **74** — **EMERGENCY PAGE!** I Can Recover From A "Food Setback"

www.MyDietisWorking.com

The emotional processes described in "My Diet Is Working! – When Traveling" do not constitute professional or medical care and should not be considered a substitute for such services. If you think you have a psychiatric or medical condition related to the theme of this book, please consult a licensed professional.

Do not use "My Diet Is Working! – When Traveling" or any dieting, eating, or body change program without prudent medical care. Use this process of discharging negative energy alongside regular visits to a doctor or other medical professional.

Do not use "My Diet Is Working! – When Traveling" to greatly speed dieting results, or to support a no-eating program or "crash" diet.

= = = = = = = = = =

TERMS USED HEREIN

– The word *diet* has been referred to as insensitive and archaic. But it is so pervasive in the field of body change that it is prominently used herein.

– Rather than the term "lose weight," the word *shed* is used because it is active, assertive, and empowering.

– The word *slender* and the phrase *become more slender* are used because they convey the strongest and most pleasant images as goal terms when shedding weight.

= = = = = = = = = =

EMERGENCY PAGE

The final page in this book (p. 74), is entitled "I Can Recover From A 'Food Setback.' " Use it to return to sensible eating, and towards getting "back on track."

= = = = = = = = = =

Also see MyDietIsWorking.com

Introduction
THE OTHER NINETY PERCENT OF BODY CHANGE

"For every action, there is
an equal and opposite reaction."
— Sir Isaac Newton

Diet book covers scream "Melt off those unwanted pounds!" – and – "Something new in the world of dieting!" But how many times have you tried their programs – only to be disappointed, again and again?

Positives, *positives,* POSITIVES! Throughout the world of body change, you are constantly bombarded by overstated, superlative messages. Most "affirmations" of traditional "Positive Thinking," of course, contain only positive words. You hope that some of their extreme claims will rub off on you. But if you achieve no results, you may feel worse instead of better.

It is estimated that *less than ten percent* of mainstream diet programs include the "underneath" side of body change – of adverse issues, feelings and emotions. The "success industry" has been criticized as hollow and ineffective.

My Diet Is Working!, however, addresses "the other ninety percent." The words of the Insights are generally positive, but most also contain a slight "edge." You may have to read them closely to sense this "gentle confront." It is designed to invite negative feelings and issues to flow through you and then clear you for preferred goals.

This is believed to be the first time such a process has ever been offered for body change. Use it alongside your favorite diet or eating program, and your favorite exercise or physical activity.

You may have tried dozens, or even hundreds, of body change programs. But now, by regular release of "negatives," you may, indeed – "melt off those unwanted pounds." And with *My Diet Is Working!*, you may have actually discovered – "something new in the world of dieting!"

HOW TO DO THIS PROCESS

You have, of course, been "processing" adverse feelings and emotions throughout your life. *My Diet Is Working!* presents this universal principle in a focused and practical way for body change:

– Strive to feel as good as possible and to acknowledge yourself for doing this useful work.

– Establish that you have eaten sufficiently.

– Breathe deeply.

– Read an Insight and let its slight "edge" gently bring up possible adverse feelings and emotions.

– Encourage these "negatives" to rise up and flow through you, in small, safe, and controlled amounts, for the purpose of release. *Your response is everything.* Remain calm, stable and centered. Guard against possibly being overwhelmed. Remember that you can stop this process anytime you want.

– *Think* of your preferred positive results, while you *FEEL* your adverse issues and emotions.

– Let the "gentle confront" of the Insight allow adverse feelings and issues to flow through you. Feel them for just a few seconds, and then let them pass out of you and dissolve. You should have a sense of moving closer to actual positive results – and you should feel better!

– Although you must feel the adverse issues very briefly – strive to do this work with overall good feelings.

– Then consider repeating this process.

– If you do not regain a sense of well-being, stop work and try again later.

– To continue the release of possible remaining adverse energy, you can also walk or otherwise move your body. Alternating left-right movement is best.

– Consider that this releasing of adverse feelings and emotions is helping you achieve your healthy weight.

(Text continued on p. 19, "Clean Out The Basement")

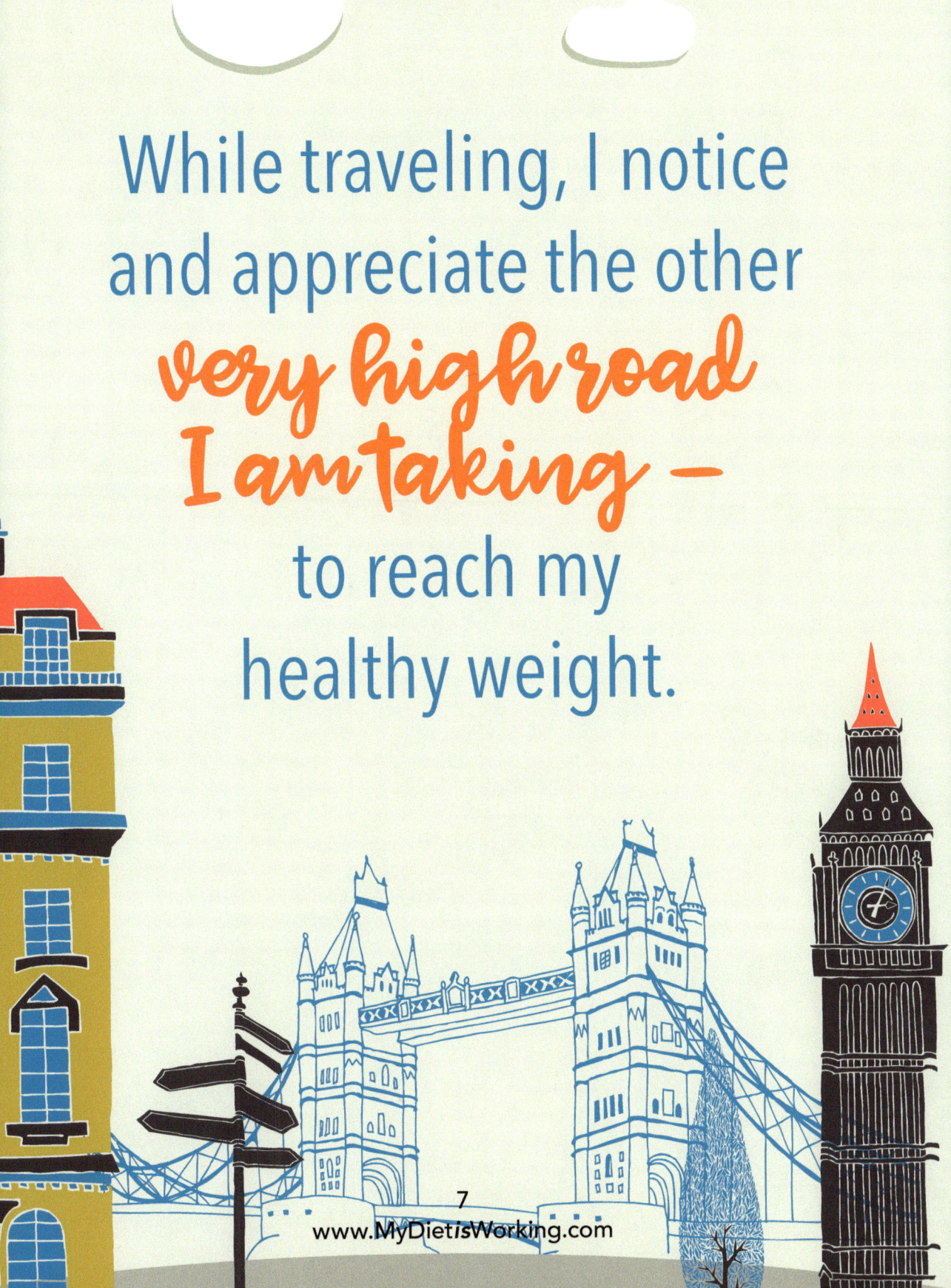

As I prepare for travel, *more and more*, I do not allow possible apprehension about *my journey* to justify overeating at home.

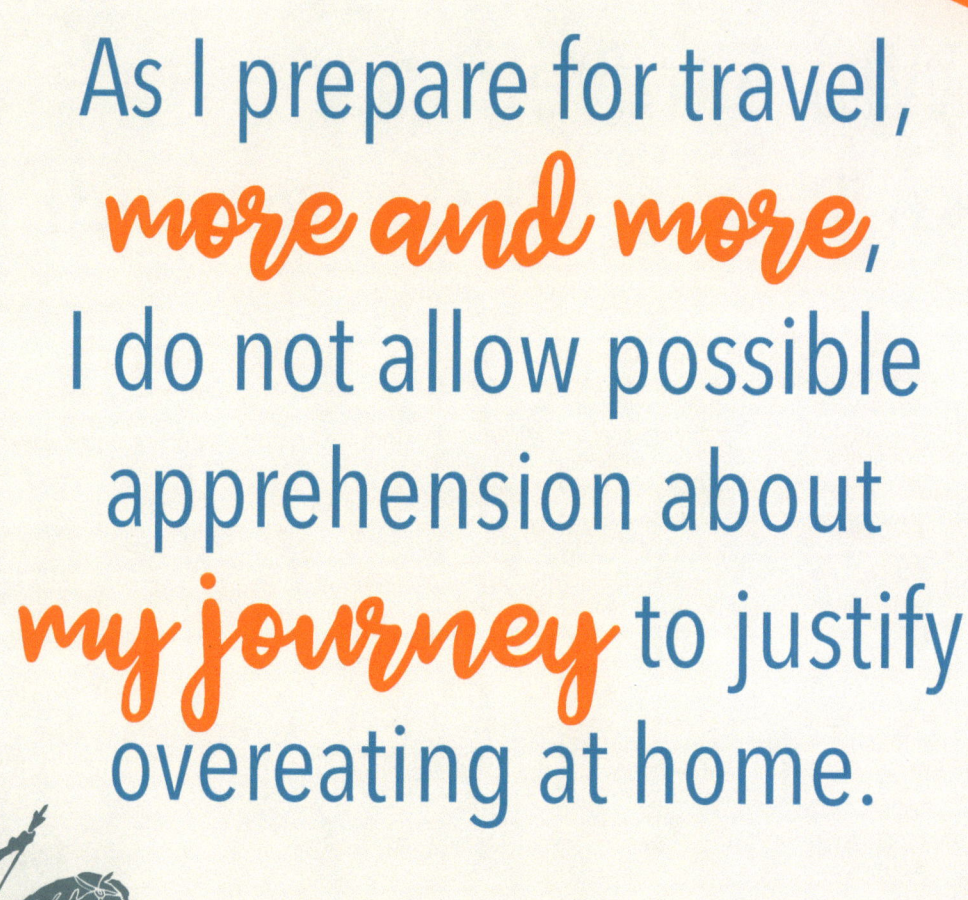

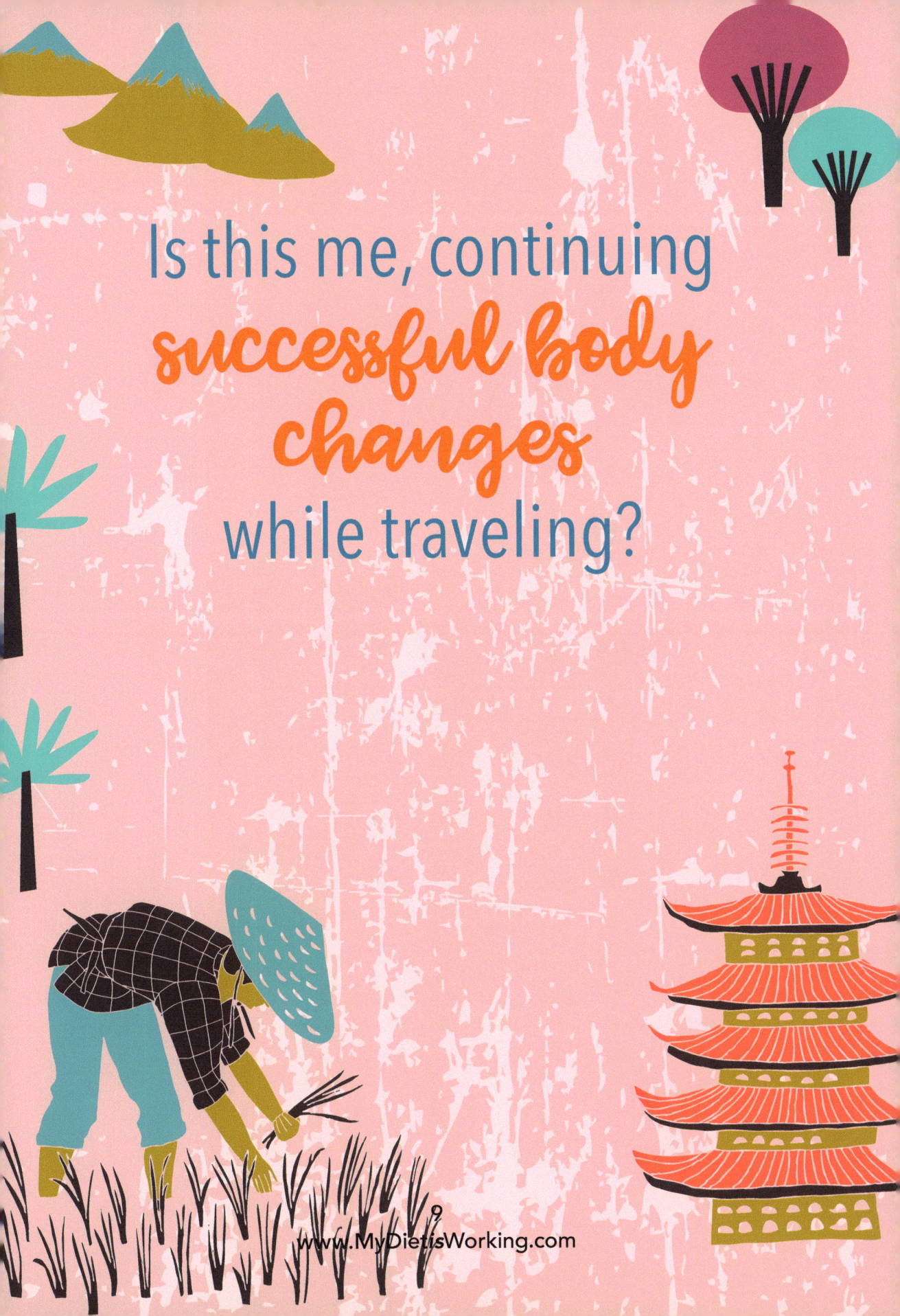

More and more, when I visit family, friends and associates, I find ways to enjoy their company *besides food.*

If I have a "food setback" while traveling, **I reconcile with myself more** "in the moment," rather than waiting until I return home.

As I travel,
day by day, I also
create more time for exercise,
personal fitness
and strength training.

I savor the experiences
of travel more, and turn compulsively to food less.

If my travels bring me to food experiences which are unusual or difficult, *more and more*, I still find ways to eat slowly and sensibly.

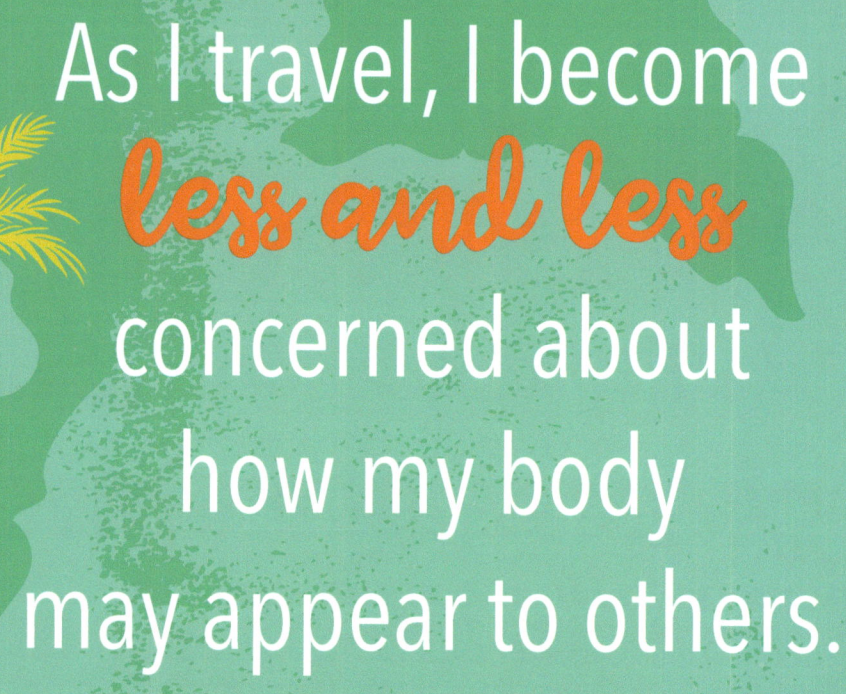

As I travel, I become *less and less* concerned about how my body may appear to others.

As I visit others, *more and more, it feels safe* and okay to be seen by them, to be visible.

As my travels bring me into unknown areas, I remind myself of *my successful* journey through another unknown territory -- of changing my body

"CLEAN OUT THE BASEMENT"

Diet success stories make it all sound so easy: "I learned how to live the principles of weight loss" – or – "My new eating plan just became a way of life" – or – "Finally I was able to make wiser food choices." But an entire other side of life is usually withheld from these testaments, and may leave you feeling as if each of these people discovered something that continuously eludes you.

All of those successful dieters had to encounter, and deal with, adverse feelings and emotions of the subconscious mind before their positive results could take place. Every one of them had to "clean out the basement" – addressed here as the release of negatives.

Real body change may be one of the most difficult things you will ever do. Almost everyone seems to be on some type of eating program.

Most Insights of *My Diet Is Working!* use the phrases, "more and more," "day by day," and other words. These are to remove absolute statements and to let your valuable negative response be easier.

(Please review *How To Do This Process* on page 6)

As you read an Insight, watch for responses like, "I don't think I would do this," "I feel resistance," "I don't like this," and possibly stronger ones. Gently let these adverse issues and emotions flow through you.

Consider this process not so much as striving for a goal, but as clearing out a space into which your preferred results can flow. As your "negatives" pass, you don't have to know exactly what they are. You can simply let them flow by. Instead of continuously fighting the same old barriers, take action to dismantle them from a new and entirely different side – to then reach the body change results you want.

Feel good – and *positive* – for taking these strong steps to improve your life! With *My Diet Is Working!*, you are facing deep issues, a segment at a time. And may "cleaning out the basement" also enable you to actually – "live the principles of weight loss."

(Text continued on p. 31, Make Friends With Repeated Energy)

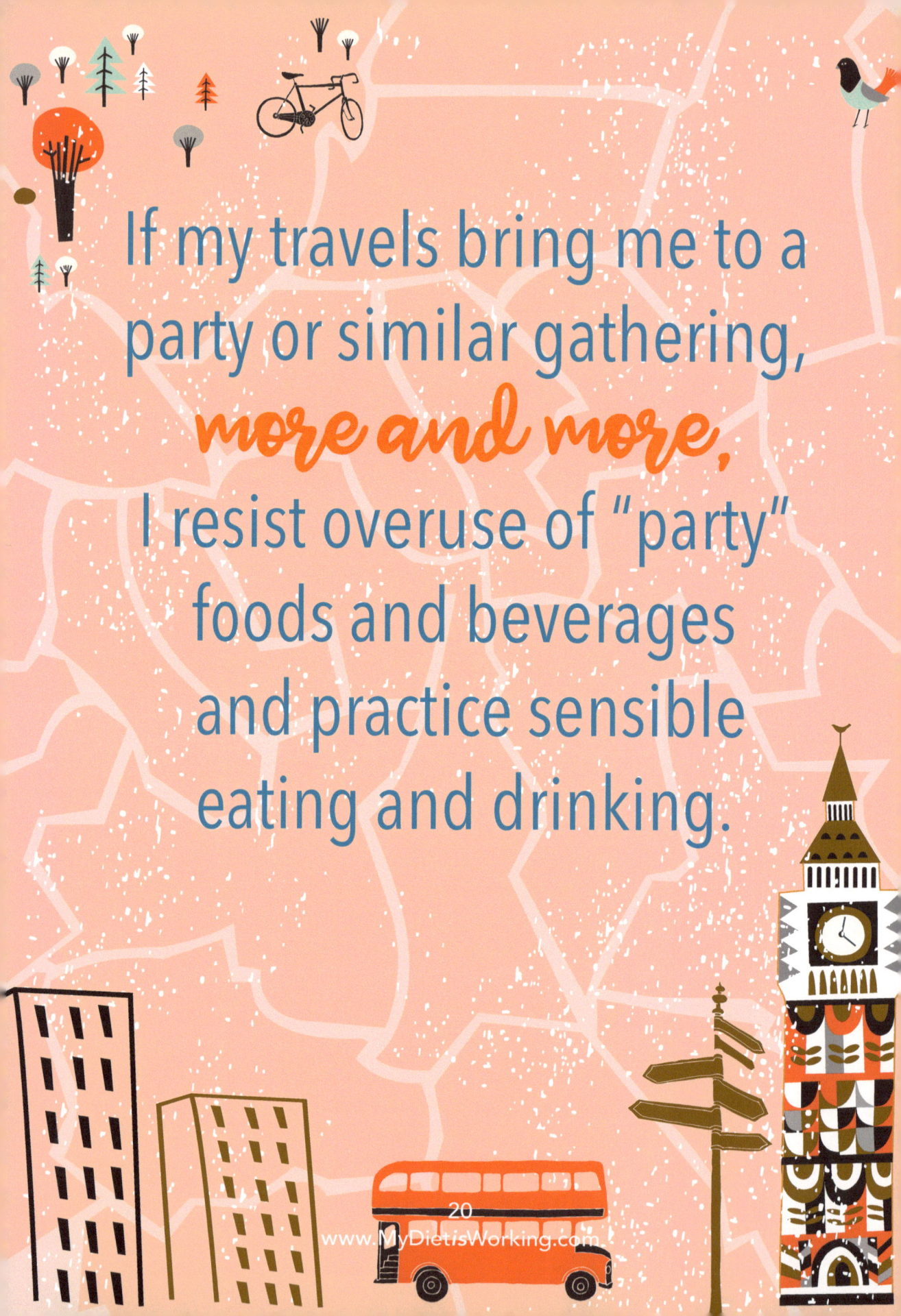

If my travels bring me to a party or similar gathering, *more and more,* I resist overuse of "party" foods and beverages and practice sensible eating and drinking.

More and more, when traveling, I keep "safe" foods and beverages available, those I can have in quantity while continuing to become *more slender.*

As I travel, I *feel safer and safer* in my body.

More and more, when traveling, I visualize sensible eating before arriving at a food experience.

As I travel, if I undergo disappointment or upset, I use food *less and less* to compensate.

When I prepare food while traveling, *more and more,* I do this as sensibly as I would at home.

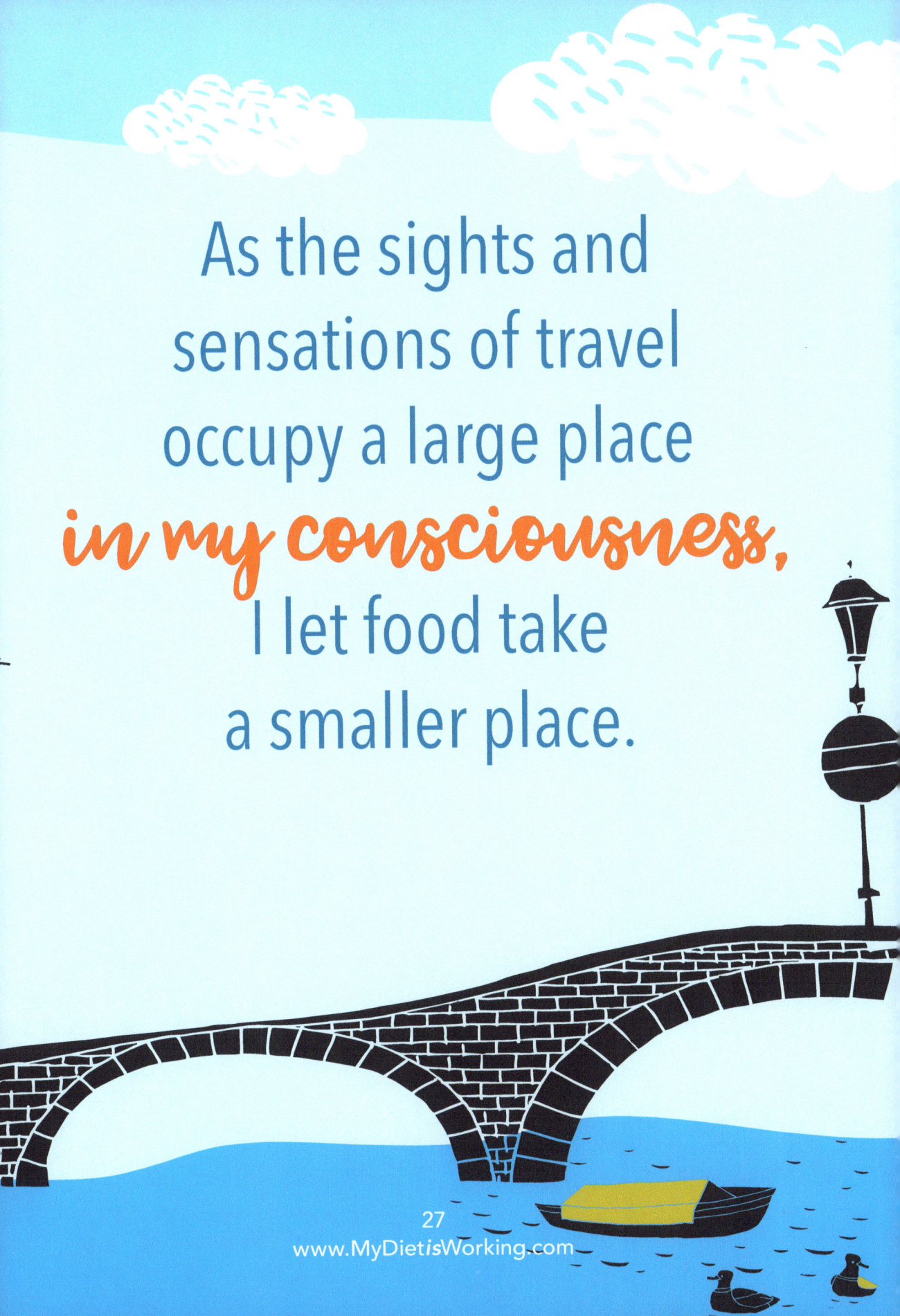

As the sights and sensations of travel occupy a large place *in my consciousness,* I let food take a smaller place.

At gatherings with others, regardless of my status, position, or rank within the group, *more and more,* I continue sensible eating.

At holiday gatherings or large food events, I feel *less and less* expected by others to eat oversize portions.

More and more, I do not judge a travel destination or experience primarily by its food.

MAKE FRIENDS WITH REPEATED ENERGY

A television infomercial promises "Shocking body truths to help you drop unwanted pounds!" But this claim, like so many others, can seem too good to be true, and they usually are.

For real body change, consider the examples of athletes, who reach their goals by dedicated repetition.

(Please review *How To Do This Process* on page 6)

As you read an Insight and allow more adverse issues to flow through you, let repetition become empowering. Consider the value in doing this process again and again. Let your continuing work become soothing, familiar, calm and relaxed.

Athletes train daily to reach serious results. They approach their workouts with methodical, ongoing energy.

Allow your release of adverse issues to become ….. gradual and metered ….. patient and methodical ….. regular and continuous.

The Insights of *My Diet Is Working!* are designed for repeated reading. As you return to their messages, watch for ongoing differences in your reactions, especially as signs of progress.

Try to appreciate your progress at any pace. Consider that you are always making progress towards your body goals, as you break up the hard work of dieting into practical segments ….. again and again.

With *My Diet Is Working!,* you are making progress in one of the most difficult things a person can do – behavioral change! Let yourself feel better! Allow these processes to help you reach *actual* positive results. And, in realizing that you are processing out stored issues, including by using repeated energy -- you may, indeed, discover -- "Shocking body truths to help you drop unwanted pounds."

(Text continued on p. 43, Try A "Bigger Shovel")

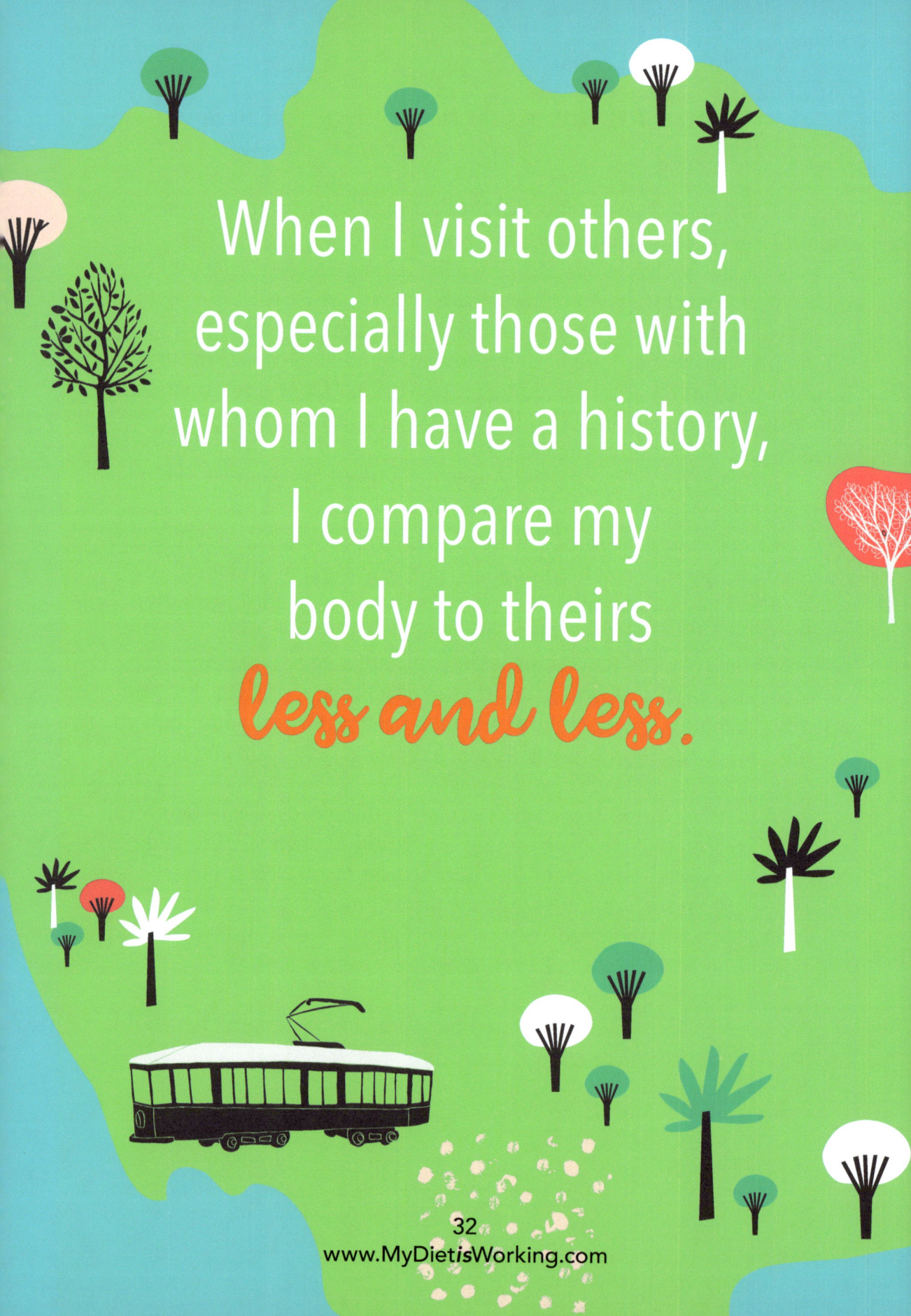

When I visit others, especially those with whom I have a history, I compare my body to theirs *less and less.*

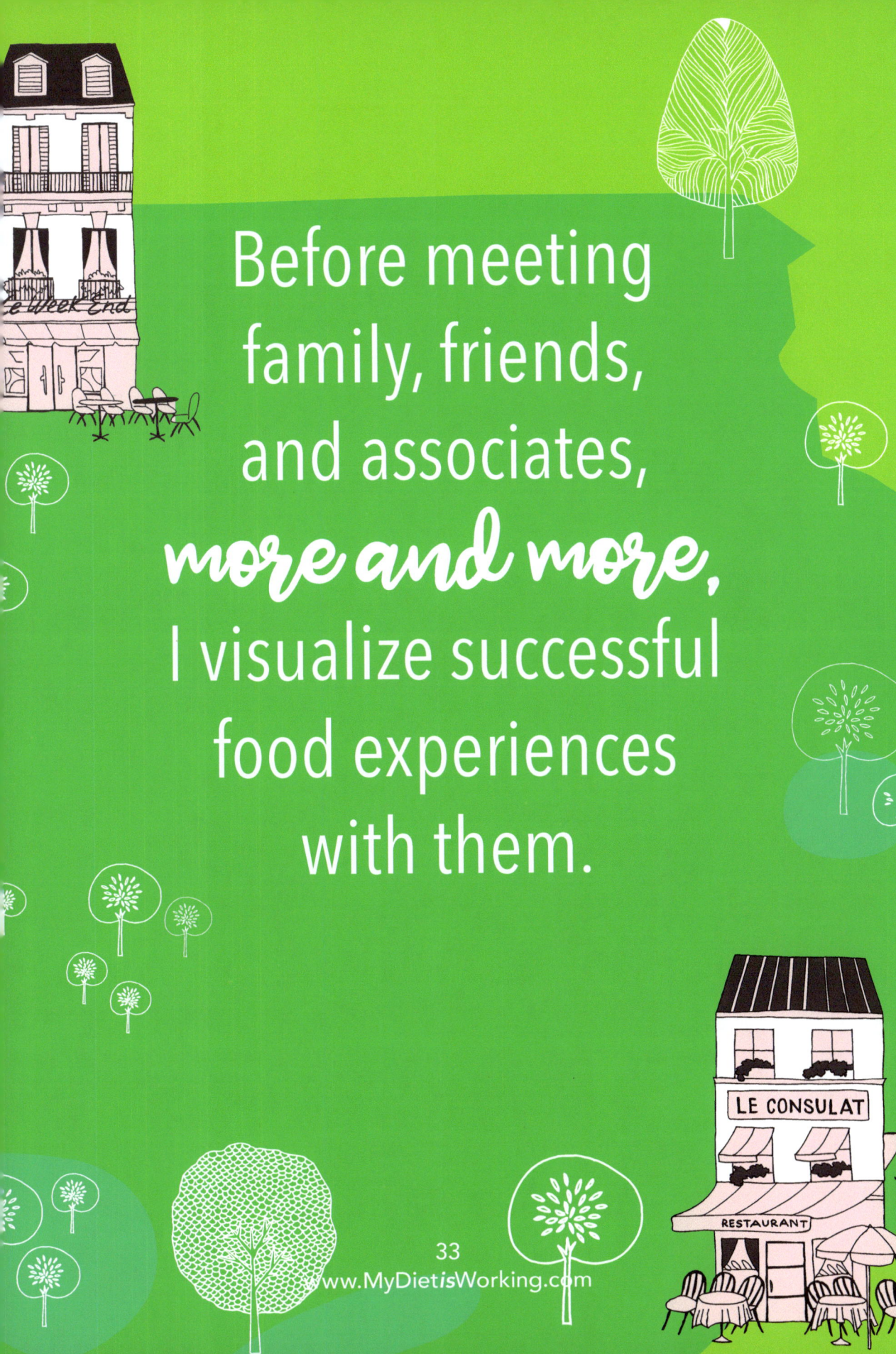

Before meeting family, friends, and associates, *more and more,* I visualize successful food experiences with them.

If, while traveling, I receive acknowledgement or praise, I use the experience *less and less* to justify overeating.

If my body has changed since I last visited others, *more and more* this is safe and okay with me.

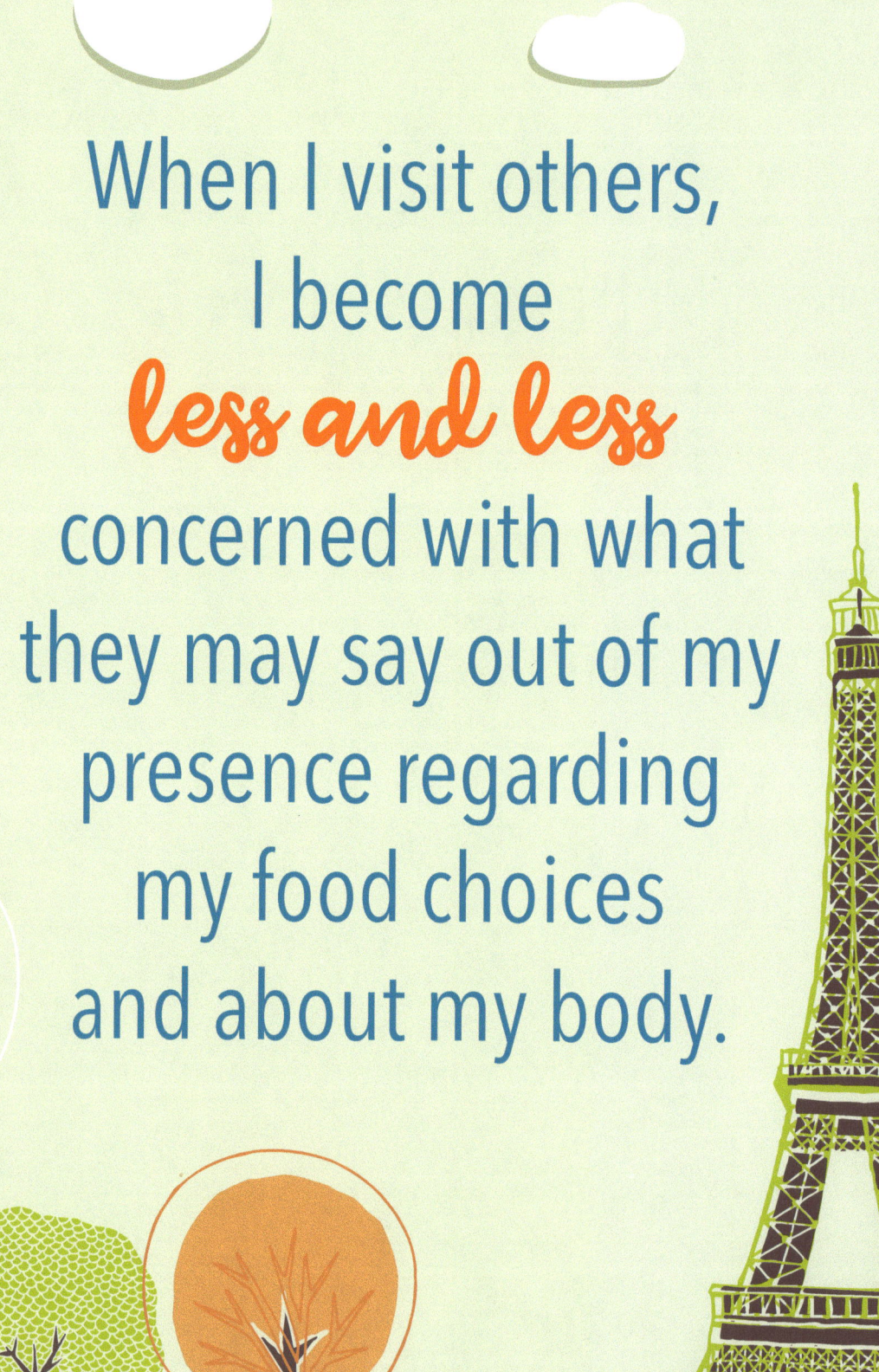

When I visit others, I become *less and less* concerned with what they may say out of my presence regarding my food choices and about my body.

More and more, I strategize my travels to avoid becoming extremely hungry.

Is this me, staying on my diet while traveling?

When traveling, *more and more,* I find ways to take breaks and to move around during meals

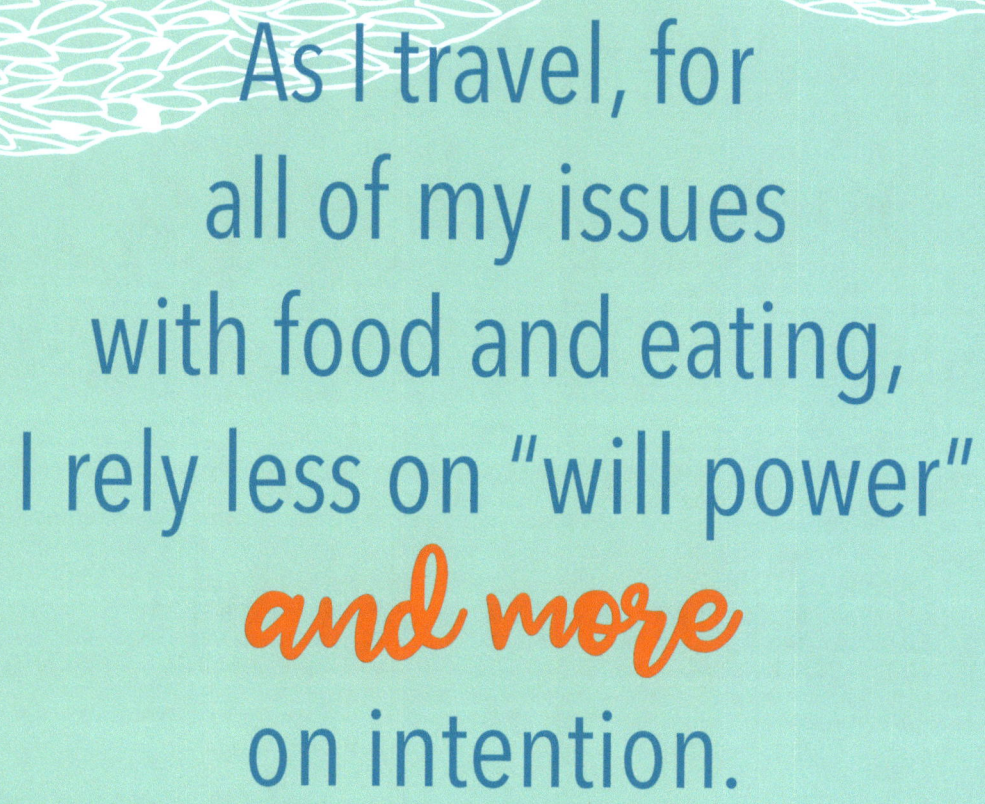

As I travel, for all of my issues with food and eating, I rely less on "will power" *and more* on intention.

www.MyDietIsWorking.com

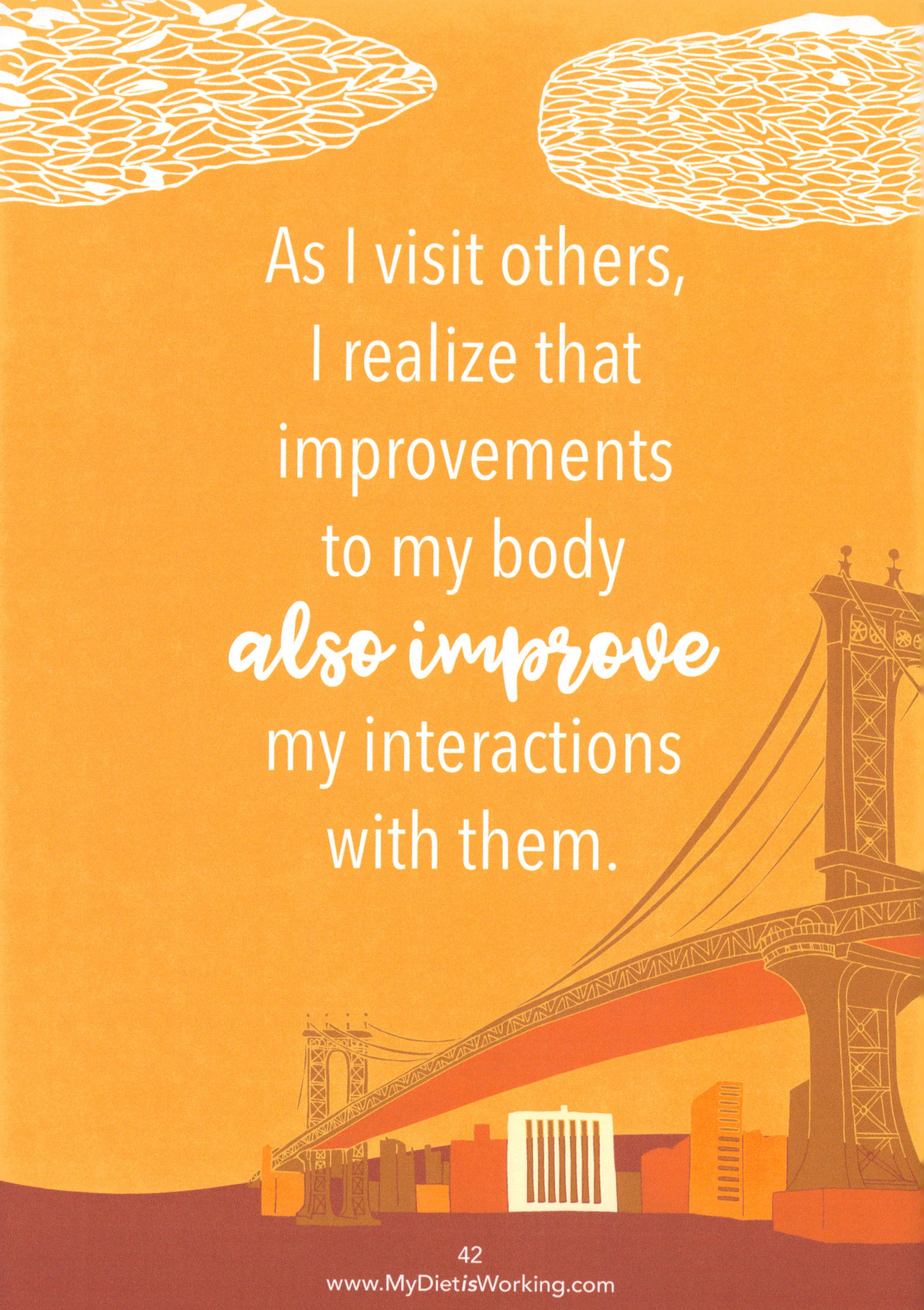

As I visit others, I realize that improvements to my body *also improve* my interactions with them.

TRY A "BIGGER SHOVEL"

As you "clean out the basement" for body change, you may also, very carefully, increase the energy of this "gentle confront" for stronger release of blocks in the way of your preferred body results.

Use the "Bigger Shovel" process only while sitting and undistracted, and after you have done *My Diet Is Working!* processing many times.

(Please also review *How To Do This Process* on page 6)

As you read an Insight, invite a stronger adverse response and allow it to build. Maintain safety as you let what may be more strenuous feelings and emotions flow through you.

If more "negatives" rise up, consider gently pushing them through you and out. Try to be more assertive while also remaining safe. You may push a bit harder, always guarding against being possibly overwhelmed, until these stronger issues pass through you to then fade and disappear.

Halt this heavier "discharge of negatives" often, to confirm your inner balance and physical safety. Take regular breaks to walk or otherwise move, preferably with alternating, left-right movements. Avoid stress and exhaustion, and increase the energy of this "processing" only in gradual amounts.

Consider that these deeper feelings, thoughts and emotions may come from earlier in your life, that they are rising up in manageable amounts, and that you are successfully "experiencing them out."

Again – take credit for doing this brave, heroic "bigger shovel" work! Watch for further breakthroughs to good feelings – and *actual* positive results!

(Text continued on p. 57, Your Further Resources)

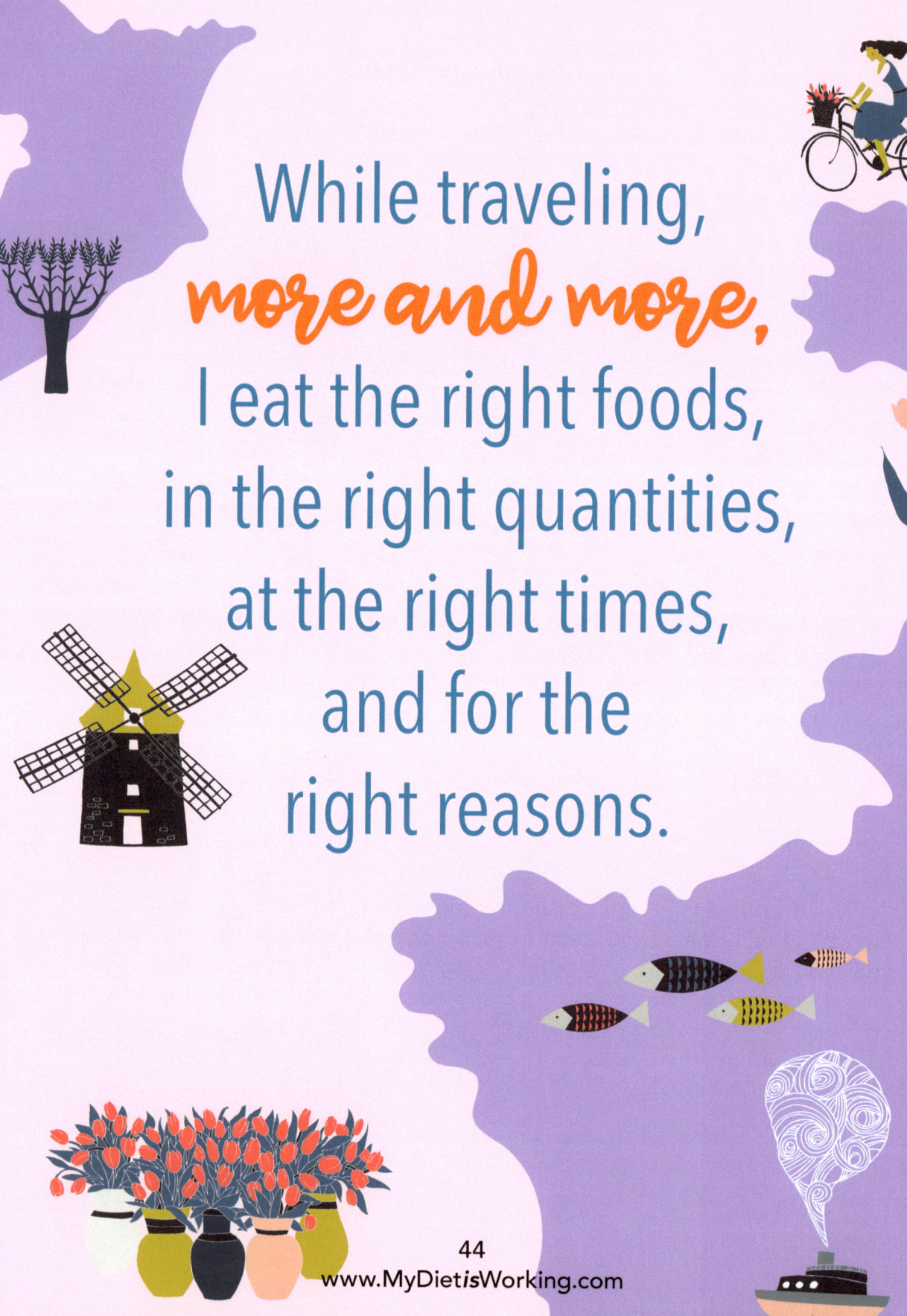

While traveling, *more and more,* I eat the right foods, in the right quantities, at the right times, and for the right reasons.

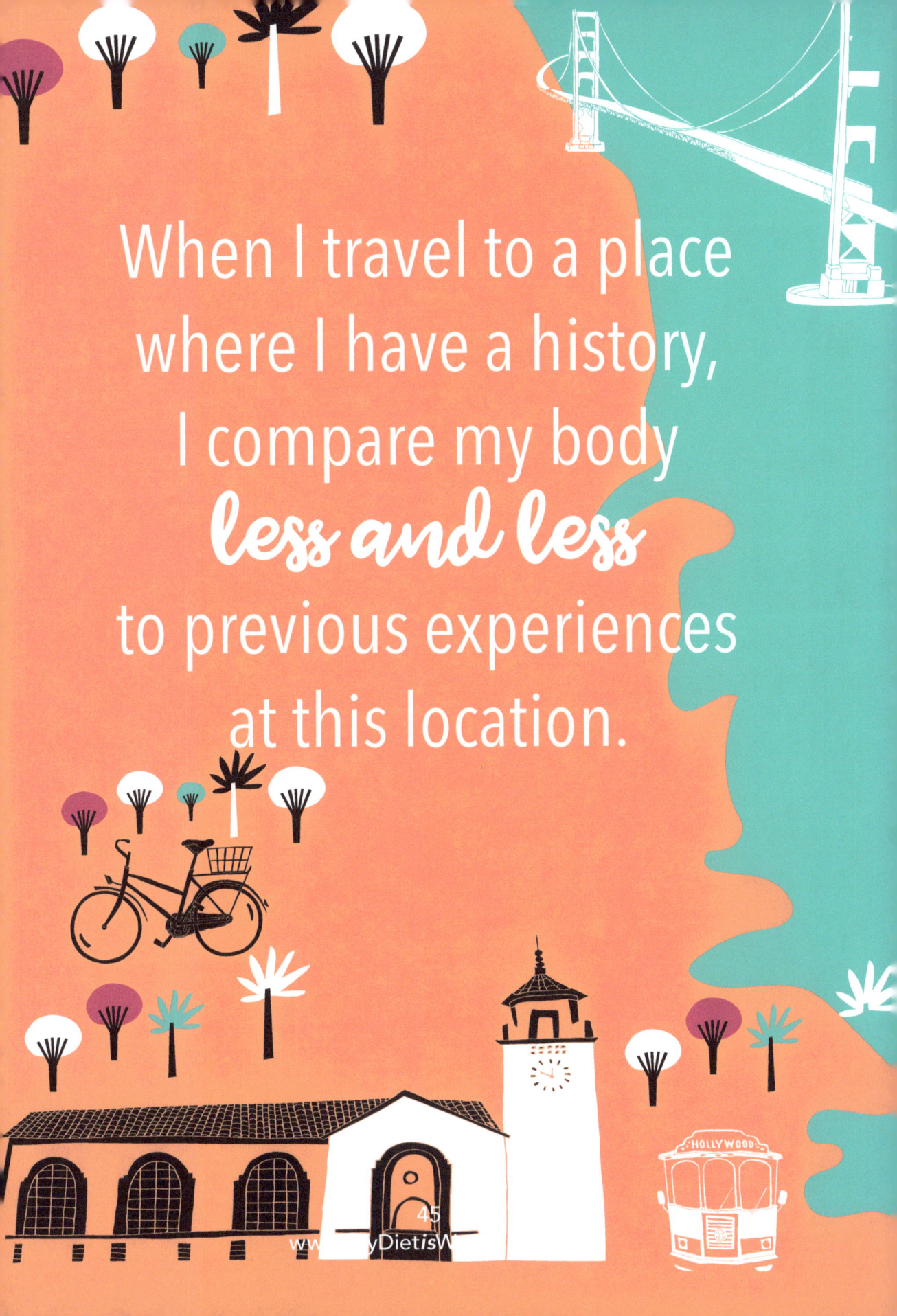
When I travel to a place where I have a history, I compare my body *less and less* to previous experiences at this location.

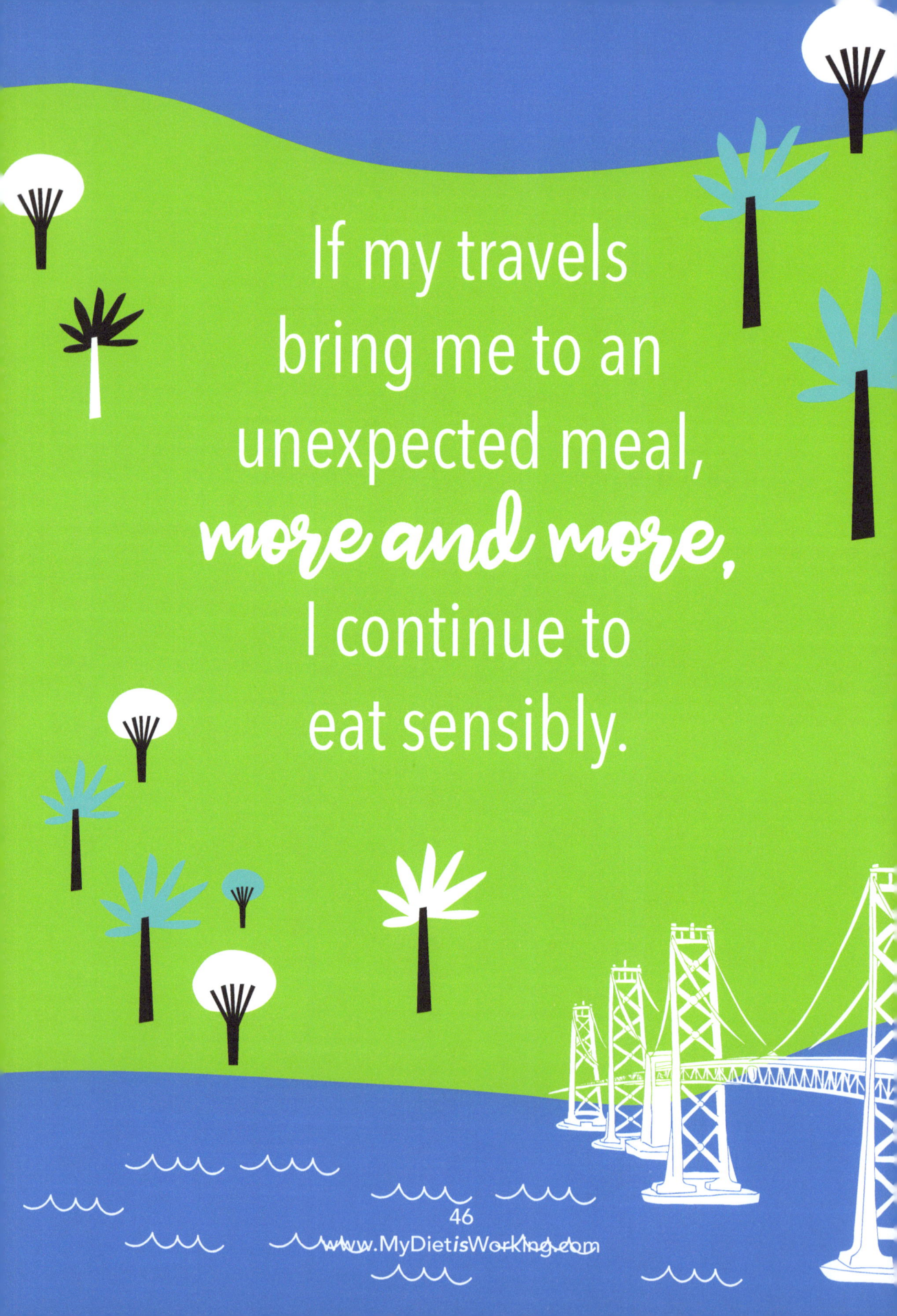

I use the special sights and experiences of travel to *remind myself* I am also making my body more special.

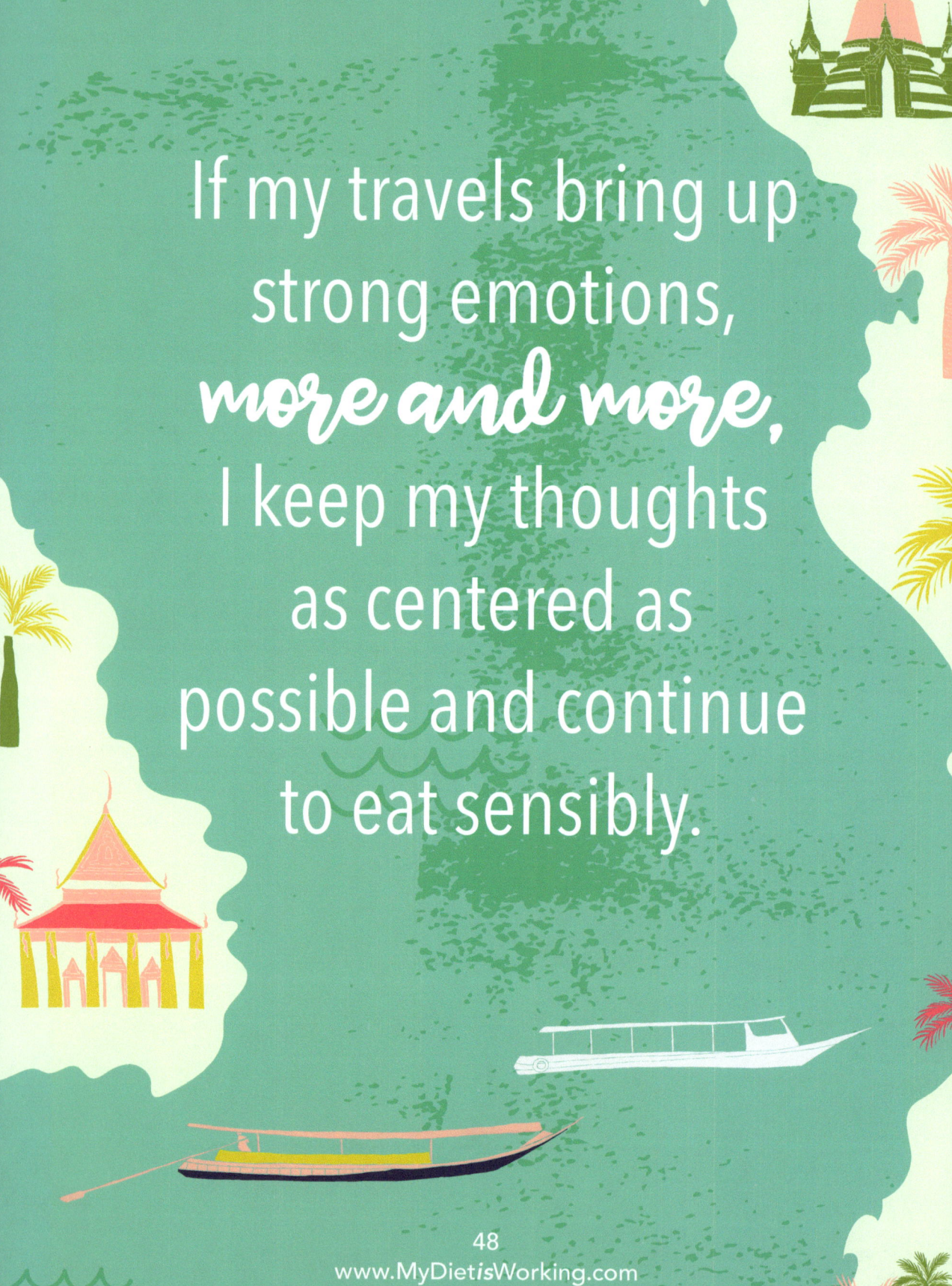

If my travels bring up strong emotions, *more and more,* I keep my thoughts as centered as possible and continue to eat sensibly.

As travel brings me to *"now,"* I remind myself that my relationship with food and eating is also happening … *"now!"*

If interpersonal issues come up during travel, *more and more,* I create ways to resolve them without using food.

I use the experience of travel **less and less** to justify eating differently than I would at home.

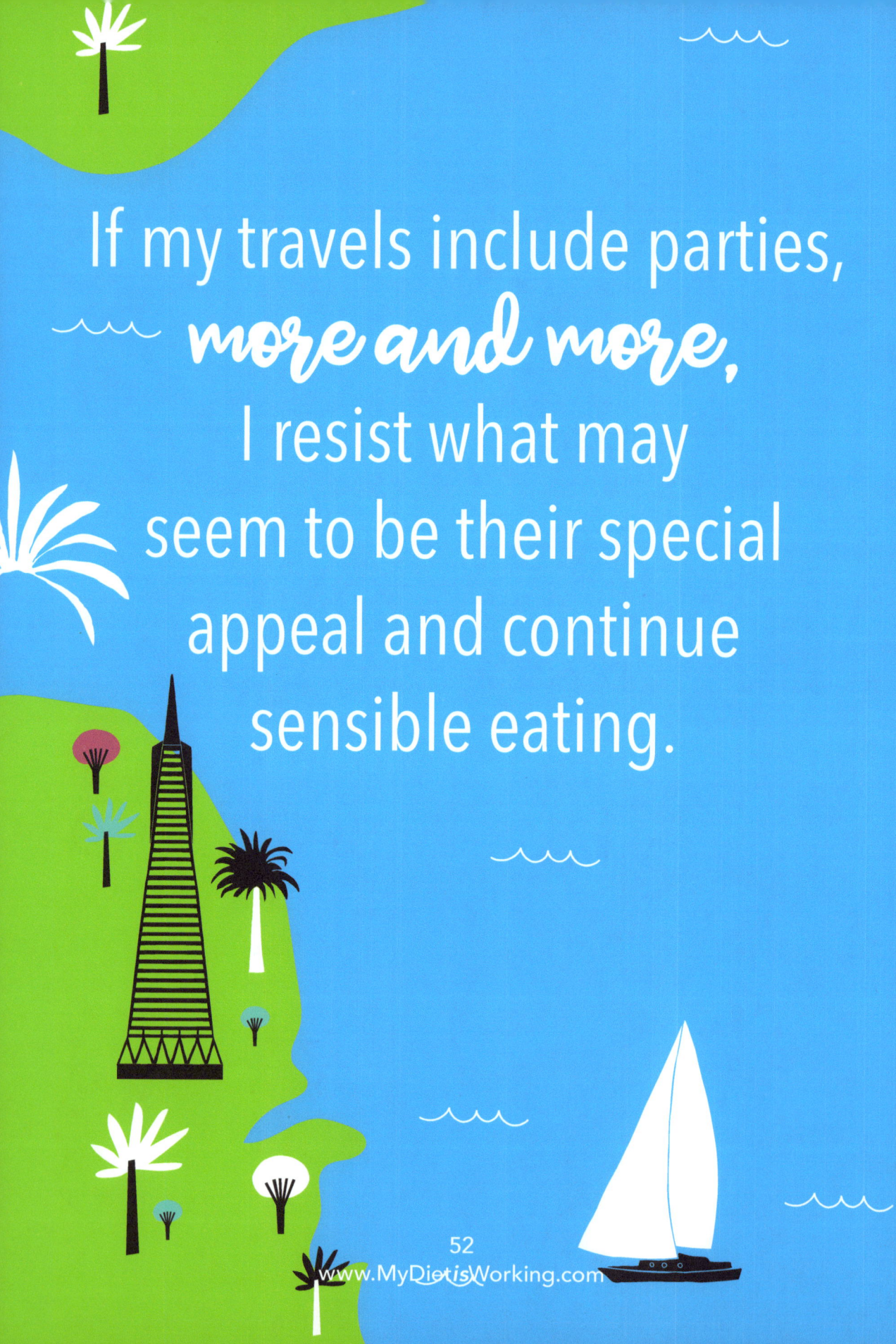

If my travels include parties, *more and more,* I resist what may seem to be their special appeal and continue sensible eating.

As travel takes me away from my regular life, *I use this imagery* to reinforce body change.

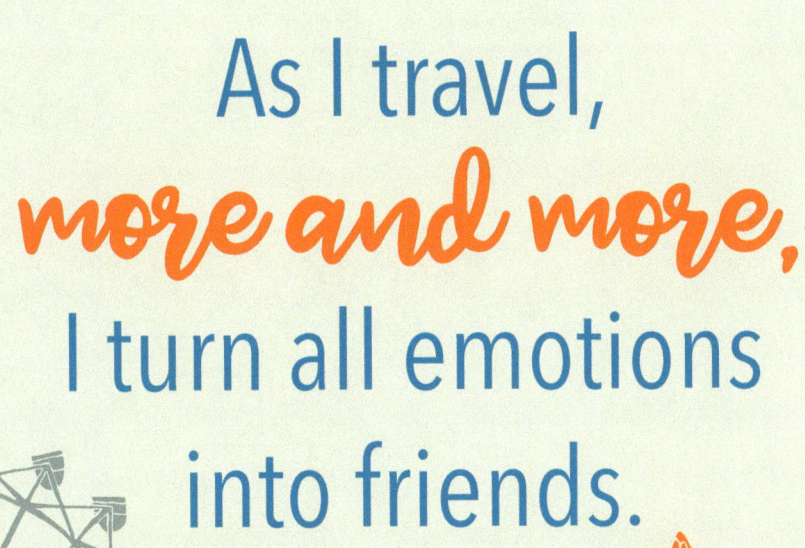

As I travel, *more and more,* I turn all emotions into friends.

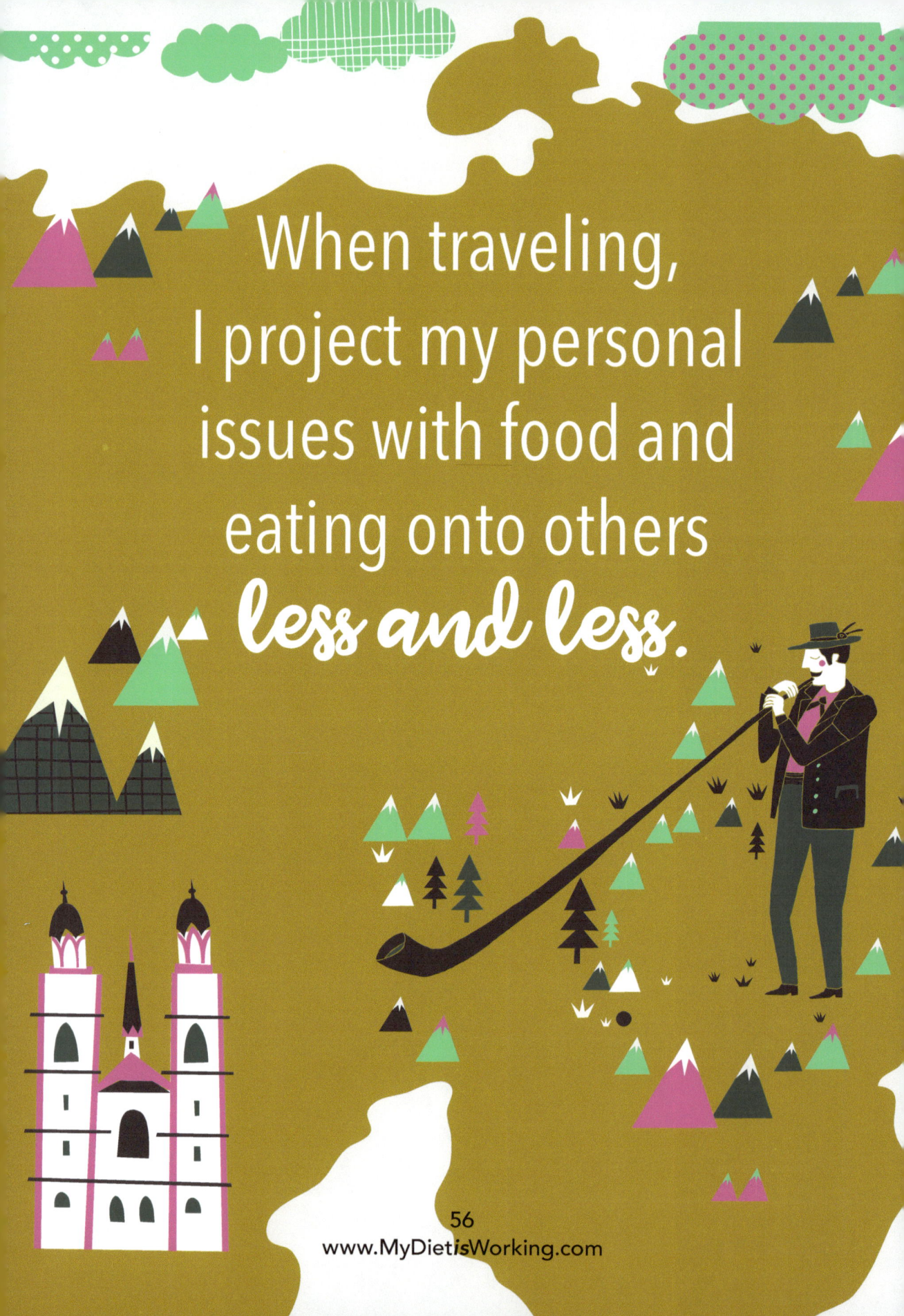

YOUR FURTHER RESOURCES

An advertisement for a weight-loss pill promises it will "give your diet a fighting chance!" But instead, consider these natural resources which are always available as you make body changes:

PHYSICAL RESOURCES: – Remain conscious of your breathing – Maintain or improve your posture – Walk or otherwise move, especially with alternating, left-right movement – Drink water to feel more full – Keep available "safe" foods and beverages, those you can have in quantity.

RESOURCES OF THOUGHT: – Appreciate and validate yourself as you are right now – Remain as calm as possible and feel your feelings – Keep your thoughts as centered as possible – Consider discharging negative thoughts and feelings as they rise up – Remain as pleasant and approachable as possible – Record your thoughts and feelings by writing, journaling or electronic means – Acknowledge that changing yourself is in fact a huge endeavor.

RESOURCES OF VISUALIZATION: – More and more, create favorable mental pictures of success with food, eating, and body change.

These resources from the world of holistic healing can help your *My Diet Is Working!* processing. And you may even discover that these natural support techniques – "give your diet a fighting chance."

(Text continued on p. 71, Conclusion)

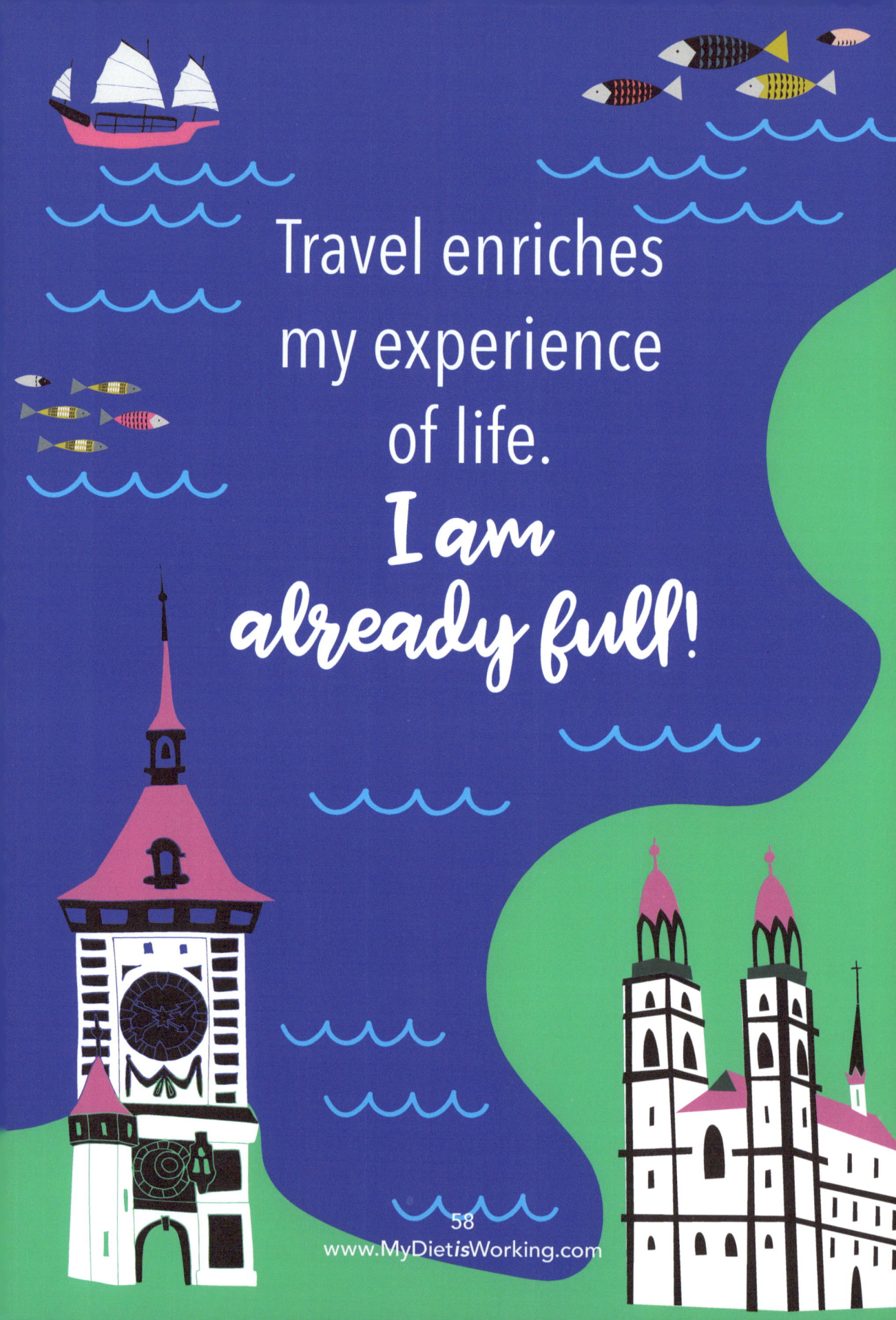

Is this me
– continuing to shed weight while traveling?

When traveling, *more and more,* I can resist the seductive lure of comfort foods.

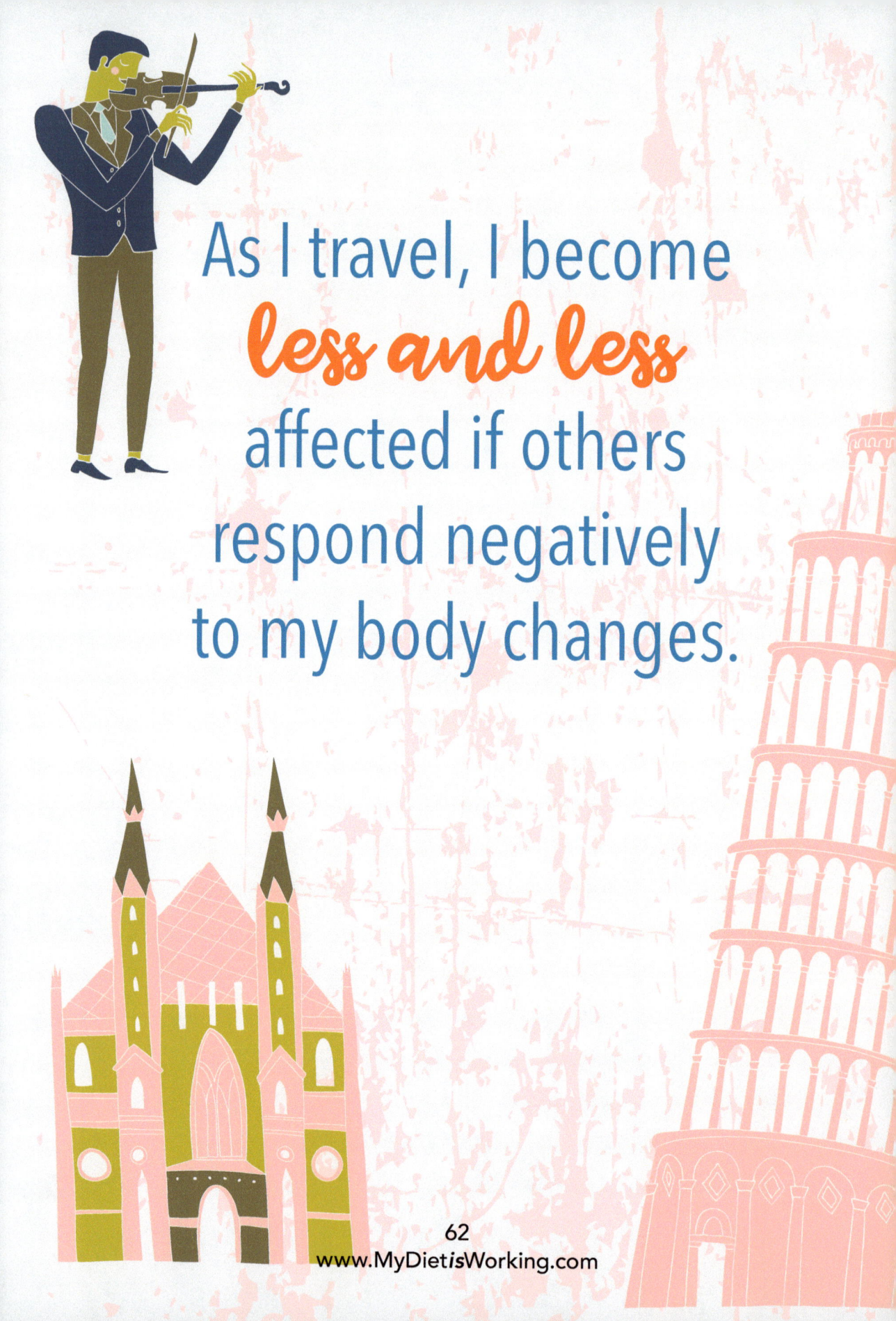

As I travel, I become *less and less* affected if others respond negatively to my body changes.

To support positive body changes while traveling, I create **more and more** time for sleep.

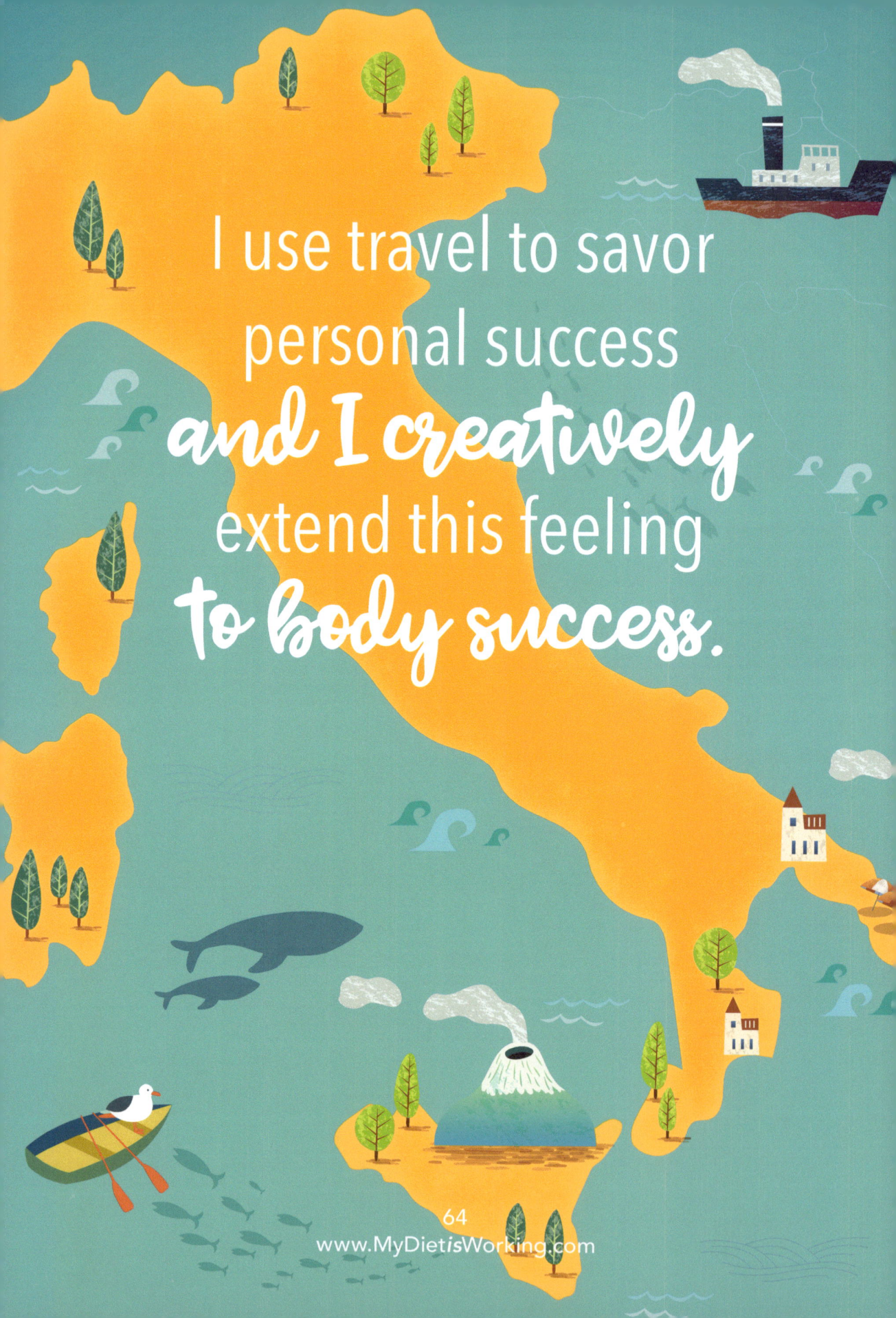

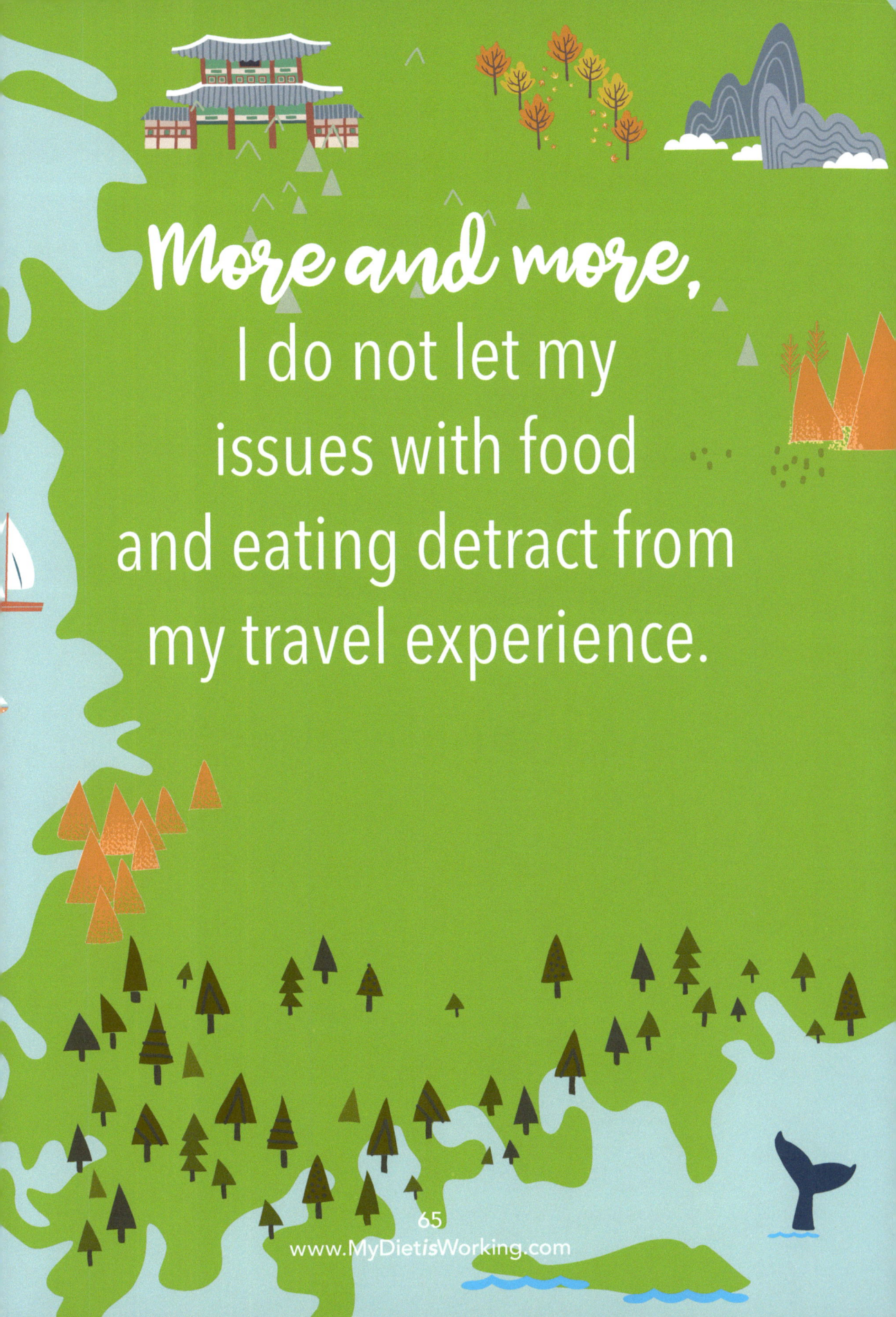

As I travel, I also maintain food awareness by **more conscientious** disposal and recycling of containers and packaging materials.

As I experience the fresh sights and sensations of travel, *more and more,* I creatively link these to positive 'body change.

Upon returning home, *I continue* to use the *positive effects* of travel to reach my healthy weight.

For all of my body goals, *more and more,* I realize that in addition to reading or listening to Insights about food and eating, I must also take physical action.

Day by day,
in every way,
my entire relationship
with food and
eating becomes
better and better.

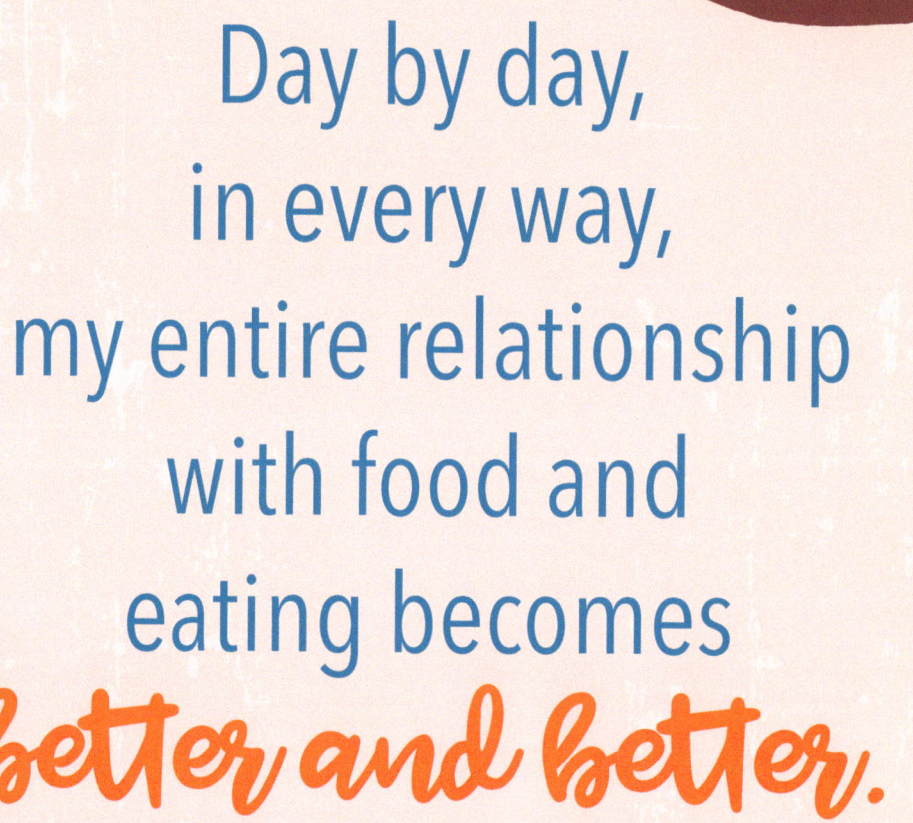

Conclusion

THE REST OF YOUR LIFE

Body change books continue to scream, "Keep the weight off, once and for all!" – and – "The last diet book you'll ever need!" But instead of their overstated, and often empty superlatives, use *My Diet Is Working!* to move toward these preferred positive results:

My body feels different ..... I appreciate my progress at any pace ..... I am taking more control of my life ..... and acknowledging that my goals are reachable ..... this attitude is empowering.

I have a feeling of taking charge of my life ..... and of winning on my own terms ..... there is something enormously liberating in facing my heavy issues ..... and in becoming bigger than they are.

This release of negatives is mechanical ..... and of bedrock practicality ..... I feel pride in doing it ..... I have more enthusiasm for the future ..... and I am tending to attract positive results elsewhere in my life.

Do this work in an atmosphere of triumph. You may, indeed – "keep the weight off, once and for all." And you may also discover that *My Diet Is Working!* actually is – "the last diet book you'll ever need."

MAKE FRIENDS WITH EXERCISE OR PHYSICAL ACTIVITY

Although *My Diet Is Working!* is a non-exercise process, it is recommended that you include physical activity in your body change program.

Exercise can too easily seem depressive or defeating. Release adverse thoughts and feelings to *prepare* for exercise or physical activity.

Focus on your resistance to exercise and let the adverse feelings flow through you, with the goal of actually including physical activity to reach your body change goals.

ACKNOWLEDGEMENTS

Editorial Input:
David Grant – Ronald A. Oaks
Geoffrey H. Tyler – Joel Hamaker

Other Input by:
Susan Carpenter – Debbie Christianson – Keri Douglas
Thom Hartmann – Laneyse Hooks
Sean & Susan Neal – Michael Pangia
Vincent Pangia – Linda Roller – Robin West
Amie Woeber – Christopher P. Wright

Illustrations by
but not limited to:
Shutterstock, Vector Stock, Lavandaart, Mio Buono, Molesko Studio, JoyImage, danceyourlife, MITstudio, Moloko88.

ABOUT THE AUTHOR

ROGER THIEL

A Washington, D.C. printer, Roger Thiel has also studied holistic health for decades.

Dismayed by the diet industry, and by what he considers to be the limitations of "positive thinking" programs, Thiel has studied dozens of other body change techniques. In reviewing human potential, holistic healing, and metaphysical growth programs, he believes their common factor is the discharge of negative energy.

He is pleased to offer *My Diet Is Working!*, as a fresh resource, focusing on the release of "negatives" as a new and different approach to body change.

An accomplished writer, dozens of his articles have appeared in aviation and other magazines. He has been featured on the History Channel for his studies of the World War Two American Homefront and is the author of a book on this theme. Thiel has conducted forums at EAA Airventure (Oshkosh) for over 30 years, most recently about Aviation Writing.

In his specialty printing business, he has helped over 3000 attorneys practicing in the U.S. Supreme Court.

Other interests include antique aviation, boating, community theatre and opera. He has announced hundreds of events including airshows, aviation pageants, boat processions, and, in his native Washington, D.C., at DAR Constitution Hall and on the National Mall.

Also by Roger Thiel:
AMERICA'S HOMEFRONT AIR WAR – THE CIVIL AIR PATROL AGAINST GERMAN SUBMARINES IN WORLD WAR II – The Untold Facts of Armed U.S. Civilians and Their Successful Lightplane Retaliation to the Invasion of America's East Coast. (2016).
See www.AmericasHomeFrontAirWar.com.

WATCH FOR THESE COMING EDITIONS
– *My Diet Is Working!* – *In Everyday Life*
– *My Diet Is Working!* – *With Processed, Convenience and Packaged Foods.*
– *My Diet Is Working!* – *And College Life*
– *My Diet Is Working!* – *And Eating Slower*
– *My Diet Is Working!* – *When Traveling – Vol. 2*
– *My Diet Is Working!* – *And The Holidays*
– *My Diet Is Working!* – *And Keeping The Weight Off*
Also see MyDietIsWorking.com

I CAN RECOVER FROM A "FOOD SETBACK"

If, while traveling, I have a "food setback" or binge, I can react consciously and positively:

– I can reconcile with myself as soon as possible, preferably "in the moment."
– I can resume sensible eating as soon as possible.
– I can review what led up to this "food setback" so, more and more, I can resist this possible pattern.
– I can eat a sensible portion of a "safe" food or beverage to remind myself I am "back on track."
– I can remind myself that despite what happened, I am still me. I still have the rest of my life. I am enough.
– I can appreciate and validate myself as I am right now.
– I can value myself for having taken the very high road of changing my body.
– I can recognize that changing my body is in fact a huge process.

– Is this me, back on track?

www.ingramcontent.com/pod-product-compliance
Lightning Source LLC
Chambersburg PA
CBHW041945110426
42744CB00027B/13